Blend Out Blogging: A Beginner's Guide to Creating a Blog, Acquiring Traffic, and Receiving Passive Income For Life

Before You Start

Congratulations for taking the first step in your journey to online success. I want to thank you for purchasing The Blend Out Blogging Book and I assure you, if you follow this guide, your success is eminent. It will be a lot of hard work to start, but when the hard part is complete, you can go live on a beach and earn money while you drink a Corona!

Before you read:

I want to make this an interactive course in which you actually achieve success. I found the best way to do so is to include little activities along the way and a checklist at the end of each section.

What you'll need:

I enjoy hand writing things versus keeping a document, but you can do either or. I would recommend keeping a pen and a journal handy for all the activities. You can also download a pre-formatted activity log book with checklists included at the following link (also included in your .zip package):

[LINK]

Note:

Any time you see this:

There is an activity that follows. I too will be doing the activity and showing my results immediately following the instructions.

That's all I have for you, so what are you waiting for? **Scroll down and get started now!**

Table of Contents

Section I – Before Starting A Blog

Before you start a blog, there are a lot of aspects to think about and it can be overwhelming. In fact, this entire guide could be overwhelming if I didn't add in checklists. Checklists will help guide you from one section to another seamlessly. I know there are some advanced users reading this that just came for a few tips, but before you jump to different sections, ensure you have everything on the previous section's checklist completed.

I created the checklists for a few reasons, but the main one is accountability. Holding yourself accountable is going to be one of the toughest things. You may become discouraged along the way due to unforeseen circumstances, lack of traffic, or the sheer work one must put in to make money online, but I assure you, you CAN do it.

It is said that only 9% of people who attempt to make money online succeed. I prefer to look at this statistic from the 9% side, because the other side of it looks quite grim. Staying positive is one of the ways I have become successful online, and I suggest you learn to do so too! There are a lot of reasons to hang your head and join the 91% who don't make a penny online, but is that what you want for yourself? Do you want to be the person who jumps from product to product hoping to catch your next big break?

Reality check: THERE ARE NO SHORTCUTS TO BECOMING RICH OVER NIGHT. ANYTHING THAT PROMISES THIS IS A COMPLETE SCAM.

There is not one magical system where one can just press "make me millions" and it does it. If there was, why the hell would anyone sell it? They wouldn't.

If you are ready to change your life, get out of your shitty 9 to 5 job and become an internet rock star in your niche, then start reading!

Choosing the Best Blogging Software

Third Party Hosted vs. Self-Hosted

There are essentially two different types of blogs out there:

1) A pre-setup blog which you have little control over such as http://www.wordpress.com
2) A self-hosted blog which you have (nearly) total control such as http://www.wordpress.org

A third party hosted blog will help you get off the ground quickly but it lacks a TON of features, the main one being the ability to monetize your website. Below is a comparison chart between the two options:

Wordpress.com	Wordpress.org
Free To Set up	Self Hosting Required
Advertisements	Control Over Ads
Limited Theme Selection	Custom Themes Available
Cannot Monetize	Earn Money
Security Measures Built-in	Plugins For Security
Limited Customization	Full Control

While there are other options for creating a blog, which I provided below, I highly recommend self-hosting a wordpress.org blog. WordPress is the most established blogging software on the market. There are tons of free plugins available that will help you along the way.

Other Third Party Automated Hosts:

1) Blogger
2) Weebly
3) Web
4) Tumblr
5) Blog.com

Other Self-Hosting Blog Options:

1) Joomla
2) Drupal
3) Umbraco
4) Pligg
5) Concrete5

Please note, those are all free alternatives to WordPress, all of which have very high reputations. But, for the purpose of this guide, I will be assuming the use of WordPress.org. WordPress is far and away the best/most established solution on the market right now. It is very easy to get started, and although there are a few flaws (security), they are easily overcome.

Knowing your Strengths is Key

As cliché as it may sound, everyone has a strength, something that they are better at than the average Joe. Playing to this strength will help you generate quality content that others will want to consume. If you are good at one particular thing, it is more than likely because you are passionate about it. Being passionate about your blogging topic is required, or you will drain yourself way too quickly. I am going to tell you a story about my personal struggle before I found success in blogging, and it something everyone may experience at one time or another; hopefully I can save you the pain.

I stepped into the internet marketing world like a lost little goat. I didn't know where to start so I just followed the herd. After finally stumbling upon blogging, I realized it was something that I was highly interested in. I absolutely love conveying my thoughts through words, and I thought it would be the perfect fit.

So, I sat down, and I conducted some research on the most popular niches to blog about. I was at it for hours when I finally found a document that gave me the following four niches: Relationships and dating, home improvement, pets, and outdoors. Out of all four, I knew that a whopping 0 of them were for me. I had little to no passion about any of those niches, but everything I had read said that you need to be in a popular niche in order to succeed. So, I decided to go with, drumroll please… **Camping**…

Mind you, I had never been camping a day in my life. I knew nothing about camping at this point, and my headline may as well have been, "The Blind Leading the Blind." But I figured that probably wasn't a good headline for a camping website, so I opted out of using it. Now, I don't want to bore you with this story, but I want you to understand how vital it is to blog about something you enjoy and have knowledge on.

Fast forward 3 months into my blogging extravaganza, I had learned all about some awesome camping recipes, but I started to become bored and tired of blogging. I saw it as a chore, and slowly I started posting fewer and fewer posts. Now, don't get me wrong, I was getting traffic and making a bit of residual income at this point, but my god was it worth it? Not at all. I dug myself a pool full of boredom and I was about to drown.

I decided to move on from the camping blog and shut it down at once. It wasn't worth being unhappy in life. Everything you do should make you happy, your "work" especially. I knew I never wanted to say, "I'm going to work" again. What I really wanted to say was, "I get to teach people about an awesome subject each and every day." I wanted to help people, but at the same time, I wanted happiness in my life, so I shut down the camping blog and went back for round two.

This time I knew I had to pick a topic which I loved, so I sat down and made a list of all the activities and hobbies which I enjoy. On my list I realized that I absolutely love two things: Learning and Books, both of which are related, as one could assume. I decided that creating a blog centered around books would be my ideal setup. Fast forward 6 months, my blog is absolutely booming! In six months' time, I built up a blog from 0 visitors to an average of 500 visitors a day, and it continues to grow. I have a list of over 1,000 people and my open rate is nearly 35%. I was able to quit my day job, and work solely on the thing I love, my blog.

The moral of the story is find something you love would love to write about, **don't force it.** Forcing it will only put you in the same place I was a few years ago. The unhappiness and the fake words will shine through and not only make it hard for you, it will repel your readers like an arachnophobist from his or her bedroom after seeing a spider inside.

Choosing the Best Niche

The above story should hold a lot of weight when choosing a niche to write in. There are so many different niches out there, and choosing one that plays to your strengths and people actually read about is essential.

Section I, Activity 1: Get out a piece of paper, and write down 10 different activities/hobbies you are interested in.

Hobbies & Interests

1. Soccer
2. Reading
3. Learning
4. Business
5. Playing the guitar
6. Music Discovery
7. Video Games
8. Working Out
9. Healthy Living
10. Sustainability

Once you have a list, it is time to narrow it down and pick the one which your blog will revolve around. You want to make sure that the niche is broad enough that you can attract a lot of people, but not too broad that you have no focus.

It is going to require a bit of research to find the right topic out of your list, but the good news is I am here to teach you exactly what to look for.

Researching your topic, step-by-step:

1) Use Google's Keyword Planner to find out how many searches there are on your topic.
2) Select "Search for a new keyword and ad group"
3) Type in the topic which you are interested in writing about, for me I typed in "Healthy Living." I then sorted the list by average monthly searches.

Your product or service

Healthy Living   Get ideas   Modify search

Ad group ideas	Keyword ideas					Download	Add all (53)
Ad group (by relevance)	Keywords		Avg. monthly searches	Competition	Suggested bid	Ad impr. share	Add to plan
Keywords like...	healthy living, ki...		407,070	Low	$2.92	0%	
Healthy (66)	healthy foods, h...		350,610	Low	$2.90	0%	
Healthy Recipes...	healthy living rec...		289,100	Medium	$1.65	0%	
Diet (17)	low fat diet, heal...		161,960	Medium	$4.50	0%	
Nutrition (32)	nutrition for healt...		95,120	Low	$3.45	0%	
Healthy Ideas (11)	healthy meal ide...		94,300	Low	$2.92	0%	
Healthy Eating (28)	eating healthy, h...		67,670	Medium	$3.04	0%	
Healthy Meals (9)	healthy meals, h...		56,320	Low	$2.42	0%	
Healthy Kids (5)	healthy foods for...		48,900	Medium	$2.58	0%	
Healthy Diet (20)	healthy living die...		41,610	Medium	$2.67	0%	
Healthy Living (200)	healthy living we...		17,320	Low	$1.45	0%	
Health Tips (37)	health tips, healt...		14,810	Medium	$1.94	0%	
Heart Healthy (14)	heart healthy livi...		12,570	Medium	$1.59	0%	
Health Food (5)	health food, heal...		11,010	Medium	$3.54	0%	
Heart Foods (17)	heart healthy foo...		9,630	Medium	$2.41	0%	

4) I am looking for a topic with low to medium competition that has a good number of searches a month, I'd say ~10,000+.

5) I decided that "Healthy Ideas" was a great place to start as it is **Low Competition** and has **90,000+ searches** every single month.

Healthy Living				Get ideas	Modify search	
Ad group: Healthy Ideas				6 of 53 ad group ideas	‹ ›	
←					Add all (11)	
Keyword (by relevance)	▼	Avg. monthly searches ?	Competition ?	Suggested bid ?	Ad impr. share ?	Add to plan
healthy lunch ideas		33,100	Low	$3.92	0%	»
healthy breakfast ideas		22,200	Low	$2.32	0%	»
healthy dinner ideas		22,200	Low	$1.96	0%	»
healthy snack ideas		9,900	Low	$3.22	0%	»
healthy meal ideas		5,400	Low	$2.61	0%	»
healthy food ideas		1,000	Low	$3.55	0%	»
healthy ideas		210	Low	$1.66	0%	»
healthy eating ideas		210	Medium	$1.75	0%	»
healthy living ideas		50	Low	$1.91	0%	»
healthy living group ideas		20	Low	.	0%	»
ideas for healthy living		10	Low	$2.16	0%	»

6) You can see that there are only 11 keywords, but they are almost all low competition. Based on this research I concluded that building a blog around "Healthy Ideas" is a good starting place, and I am quite interested in doing so.

If you are struggling to come up with an idea for a blog and none of your hobbies/interests are going to work, there are a few different resources you can use to find a suitable topic.

1) **Clickbank** – Clickbank is an information product resource which sellers can upload their products. You can use the "marketplace" on clickbank and do some research on products that are being sold.

2) <u>Amazon</u> – There is no doubt amazon is the online retail juggernaut of this generation. You can skim through all the categories that Amazon has and if any catch your eye, write them down and do the research I showed you above!

3) <u>Google Trends</u> – Google trends is a way to see what people are most searching for. This will give you a list of all the hot ticket topics, just make sure they are going to be around for a while. For instance: you wouldn't want to make a blog revolving around one movie.

4) <u>LongTailPro</u> - Long Tail Pro is a keyword tool which will help you generate keywords for your broad niche. It will find low competition keywords which you can build a blog around and it is highly recommended!

Section I, Activity 2: In your notebook write down: **Your broad topic, your narrow topic, the competition threshold, number of monthly searches, and 5 keywords of your narrow topic.**

```
#9 Healthy Living
                    Healthy Ideas - Low Comp & 99,300 searches
      Key word                    Avg. Searches
1. Healthy Lunch Ideas            33,100
2. Healthy Breakfast Ideas        22,200
3. Healthy Dinner Ideas           22,200
4. Healthy Snack Ideas             9,900
5. Healthy Meal Ideas              5,400
```

Being a Driver, Not a Passenger

Motivation... Being able to motivate yourself from within can be the difference between being worth $1,000 or being worth $1,000,000. It can be the difference between you being in a short term relationship or a long term marriage. The point of the matter is, is that our lives, the world we live in, can be dramatically influenced by either being a driver (motivated) or a passenger (unmotivated). The drivers of our society, our neighborhoods, politicians, celebrities are making advances in their lives while the passengers simply sit back and live by curiously. Our DNA is designed to be constantly stimulated. The second we lose interest in what we are doing we simply lose motivation and or desire to become something greater than we could have ever imagined. Do you feel like you are a driver that simply needs more fuel to keep moving forward? Not sure how to break the cycle of being a passenger? I want to be the fuel that takes you to the next part of your life.

Your life on Earth is important to me. Why? Because I have been fortunate enough in my life to have experienced being both a passenger and a driver. By sharing my experiences, my life choices, and what I have learned throughout my life I hope to make a difference in yours. What I am going to teach you isn't rocket science, you won't have to create the Sistine Chapel but by simply implementing key concepts that have taken me years to learn you will begin to achieve anything you could have ever imagined possible. My goal isn't to promise unrealistic expectations. My goal is to deliver essential tools that can dramatically push you to marching down paths you never thought were possible. Imagine a world where nothing could stand in your way. A world where you can create your own happiness, your own success, your own relationships. There is only one thing standing in between you and a world you have only dreamed about. Look in the mirror. It's you.

Becoming a driver means you need to put yourself around other drivers. It's that easy. If you are aspiring for greatness in all aspects of your life then you need to surround yourself with people who have already made that choice or are in the process of moving towards becoming a driver in the area's you are looking to excel in. As a kid I grew up in what most people would consider a wealthy neighborhood. Most of my friends at the time had no reason to achieve anything other than what their parents, CEO's of major corporations I might add, would give them for allowance. Being financially motivated (a driver) I could never seem to relate to people my age where I grew up. While they wanted to go out and party I often times found myself being a passenger in a place that I knew I never wanted to become a driver in. Instead, I found myself talking to other drivers who were years older than me who were striving to achieve goals that I had always wanted to achieve.

This concept is what I call "Breaking the Trend". The best way I can describe this concept would be to talk about salmon. During the fall salmon like to swim upstream. Anyone who has ever swam upstream or witnessed someone else swim upstream knows just how difficult that can be. To be honest, it makes absolutely no sense why a salmon would decide to swim against the water when it could simply swim with the water, a safer choice with less chance of getting hurt. Same principle applies with our lives. The fish that decide to swim with the current (passengers) are the ones taking the easier option. This is an option that is being chosen for them and that they are refusing to go against. The fish that decide to go up stream (drivers) are the ones that are going against common sense and are what I would consider, breaking the trend. Not everyone needs to "Break the Trend" to be successful, however, I have never met a person in my life who hasn't had to make a difficult choice against a crowd.

So how do you "Break the Trend" in your life to go in a direction you would feel is more desirable? Any trend you try to break will not be easy. Some trends may be easier to break than others but for the most part you will be going against something your body has been trained to accept. You will first need to accept that you are not happy with the situation you are currently in. The sooner you can accept that you're not happy the sooner you are ready for a change and the quicker you will be able to get out of your current situation. The best trend breakers are not the ones that rationalize the direction they are currently going but are the ones that visualize a direction they want their life to go. They then begin to accept that they will have to make sacrifices to achieve that visualization. Remember, nothing worth striving for is ever simple to achieve. Once you have come to terms with your current position in life you are ready to start breaking your trend.

Section I, Activity III

CURRENT POSITION REALIZATION ACTIVITY

For this activity to work DO NOT move forward to the next

number before completing the number you are on!

1). Write down <u>ONE</u> area in your life that you feel you are a

passenger in. This should be one or two words such as:

Marriage, Business Finances, etc.

----------------COMPLETE QUESTION 1 BEFORE MOVING ON--

----

2). Under the word you have chosen write down 5-10 bullet

points for why you feel that you are a passenger in this area.

----------------COMPLETE QUESTION 2 BEFORE MOVING ON--

----

3). Re-read all 5-10 bullet points and put a star next to the 2 TOP

reasons

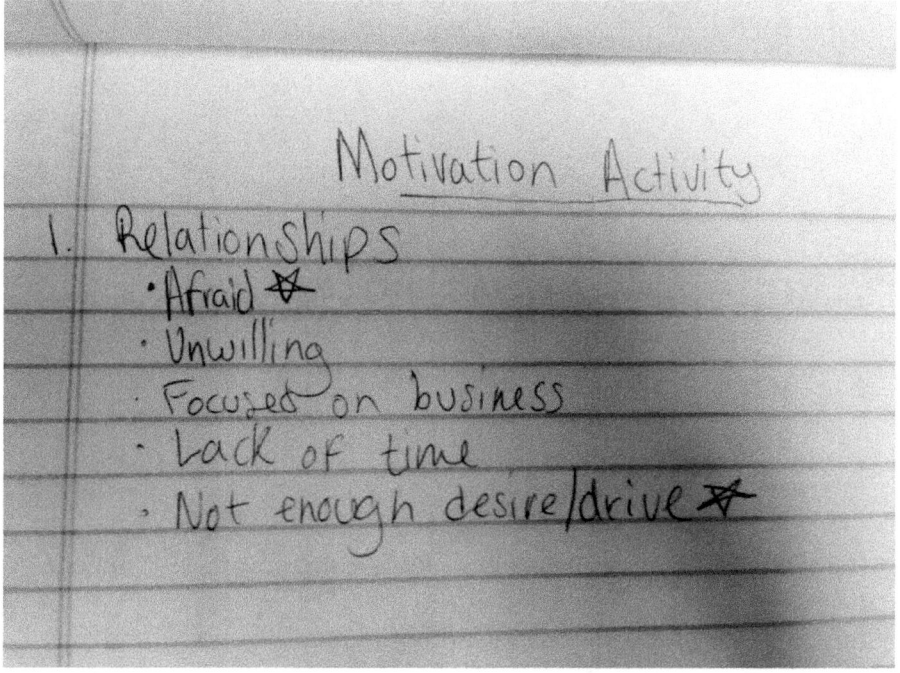

If you were able to list an area in your life that lacks what you are

wanting, were able to list 5-10 bullet points for why it lacks where

you would like to be and could star 2 top reasons that stuck out to

you, then you are ready for the next phase. Studies have shown that

the 2 top reasons with stars are within the first 5 bullet points. What

this tells us is that subconsciously, as humans, we are more likely to

write down the bigger reasons for not being happy sooner than reasons that aren't as important. Keep in mind that the two stars you have on your paper are the REAL reasons you are ready to break the trend in your life.

ACTIVITY COMPLETE

After completing the previous activity you are now well engaged with the area in which you are wanting to break the trend and are ready for the next step. The next step is as simple as it sounds, you need to break the trend. Whatever it is that is keeping you from where you want to be will need to be cut off from your life. Nothing worth getting is ever easy to achieve. If you are feeling uncomfortable then this means you have picked a trend worth breaking. If you take at least one thing away from this section I hope it is that you are learning how to say no to being a passenger and are now able to say yes to being a driver in your life. Life is short. It is short for those that are passengers in lives they dread when they could have been driving the life they have always dreamed about. It's that simple yet so many of us start to realize this lesson towards the end of our life.

How can this relate to blogging? Chances are you picked up this document of words to figure out an easier way to become rich. In a sense you have already started to break a trend in your life by trying to educate yourself towards taking a smarter path with stability in your finances. I wish that this world didn't revolve around money, but in a sense, it unfortunately plays a role in everyone's life. The biggest motivator in your life is you. The second force that will motivate you are the people you surround yourself with. If you surround yourself with people who are negative or don't have good intentions for you then you are better off being alone. Create an environment for yourself that screams success. Put yourself in situations you normally wouldn't so that you can become a better person. Are you going to look back at the end of your life and wonder why you didn't do something or are you going to be the person that looks back and realizes you have done everything you ever wanted to do? It doesn't take a genius to figure out which one most people would choose but this is the time in your life when you need to make that choice. Stand up for what you want in your life and be a driver, not a passenger.

Frequently Asked Questions before Starting

Do I need to invest any money to start a blog?

Yes, and no. I would suggest having a bit of initial capital in order to cover what you'll need in Section II (Domain name, web hosting, template). But, if you wanted to start a blog without capital you could use the resources I suggested in "Choosing the Best Blogging Software."

Is blogging for everybody?

No, it definitely is not for everyone. Blogging requires time and effort as well as a passion to share your knowledge. If you absolutely hate writing, I would suggest staying away from blogging. That being said, there are solutions such as vloging (video blogging) for those who despise writing.

Is it realistic to create a profitable blog or is it only the select few who succeed?

Well, it really is only the select few who succeed, but not for the reason you may think. The select few who actually do create a revenue stream from blogging did not "luck" into it. In fact, there was little to no luck involved. Those people sat down, put in the time and effort, and continued to push through the hard times until they achieved success. You too can achieve success if you are mentally prepared and want it badly enough. Follow this guide and I assure you, you will become successful.

How long will it take to start earning any sort of money?

Honestly, it depends on the tactics you use to acquire traffic. If you paid for traffic, you might see results the next day. If you are just using white hat SEO methods, it could take a few months before you start earning money, but once the flood gates open, you'll earn a lot!

Section I Checklist

1) I know my strengths are:

    a.

_____

    b.

_____

    c.

_____

2) I wrote down 10 niches that I am interested in   ☐
blogging on.

3) I narrowed my list down to one option and chose the
following niche:

    a.

_____

4) I conducted keyword research on my niche to help   ☐
narrow it

  down.

5) I narrowed my broad niche down to the following:

    a.

_____

6) I completed the motivational activity and I'm ready to get

   started! □

Section II – Setting Up Your Blog For Success

Choosing A Winning Domain Name

Now that we have our niche selected, keywords written down, and we're ready to start building our blog, we have to choose our domain name. A domain name is the URL for your website, IE: www.google.com.

Choosing a quality domain name is not as important as it once was. Google is not rating keywords in domains as highly as they once did, therefore you have some room to play. I still would come up with a domain that is relevant to your niche and makes sense. There would be no point to have a healthy living blog and call it Soccer Players United…

On to the fun part, keywords! This is going to take some imagination and effort, don't jump the gun because you're anxious, make sure it is what you want. It will stick with you for the life of your blog!

Write down a list of words that you would consider having in your domain name. Categorize the words and mix/match them to discover your new website name!

Healthy Ideas

Main Keyword(s)	Supplemental Keyword	
- Healthy Ideas	- Cooking	- Living
- Healthy Recipes	- Recipes	- Lifestyle
- Health Freak	- Ideas	- Guru
- Healthy Cooking	- Freak	- Lunch / Dinner
- Healthy		
- Health		

Action Keywords

- Fast	- Now
- Get	- Easy
- Become	- Quickly
- Forever	- Results

- Healthy ideas. com	- Health Guru. com
- Healthy cooking ideas. com	- Healthy Lunch Recipes. com
- Healthy recipe ideas. com	- Healthy Dinner Recipes. com
- Healthy Living Ideas. com	- Healthy Cooking Recipes. com
- Healthy Lifestyle. com	- Health Freak Ideas. com

As you can see, I stuck with my niche from Section I. I have written down a list of keywords I felt were relevant to my niche, and also used some of the keywords which I found on google keyword planner. I provided a list of action words which you can use if you are struggling to find a domain without them. For instance, if I wanted healthylifestyle.com and it was taken I could add healthylifestyleforever.com or something of that sort.

I came up with a combination of 11 different domain names and now I am going to check their availability using GoDaddy's Bulk Domain Tool.

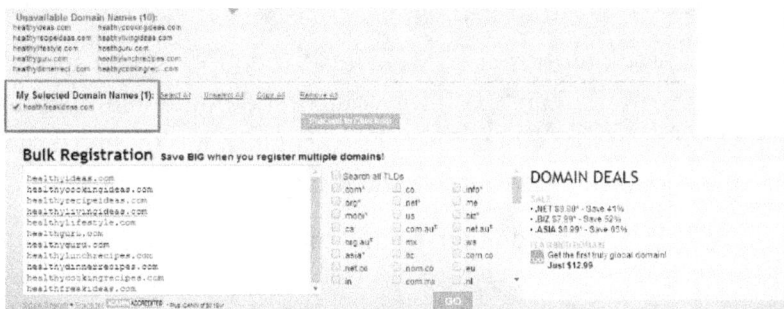

I checked all 11 domain names at once using GoDaddy's tool. A whopping ten out of eleven domains were unavailable, but that means one was. I don't mind the name that is available and I would consider using it if I could come up with nothing else. I wrote it down and I crossed off the unavailable ones.

It is a process which will take time, but you will eventually come up with the perfect domain name, it is out there. You can use other extensions, though the only other one I would suggest is .net.

Purchasing your domain name is really easy.

Convenient Method:

The easiest method for purchasing a domain name would be through your webhost which you will find in the next step. It may be a few extra bucks but you won't have to deal with switching nameservers, which for someone new can be a pain!

Inexpensive Method:

I would stick to GoDaddy because they are very inexpensive and highly reliable. Once you have found the one you want, travel back to their homepage and complete the purchase.

Two websites for coupons:

RetailMeNot

FatWallet

Be sure to look at those two websites for coupons, you shouldn't be paying any more than $5.00 for your first domain name. Ignore all the added crap that GoDaddy tries to suggest to you, most of it (if not all) is pointless for a first time blogger.

Best of luck on your domain search and I'll see you in the next chapter.

The Best Webhost

I am going to be honest from the get go here: the best web host can be extremely opinionated, but I have extensive experience with two, so I will share both, but first let me explain why you need web hosting.

Web hosting is where all of your WordPress files will be hosted at in order for people to see your website. It is required if you want to host a WordPress blog to have web hosting. Again, you can avoid the expense of web hosting if you refer back to Section I where I noted a few hosts that are free, but I wouldn't recommend it.

Bluehost:

Bluehost is far and away the most popular web hosting amongst internet marketers and bloggers. It is a fantastic host because of their support and quality of hosting received, all for a very low price. You will pay around $4.00 a month with Bluehost, and I assure you, it is worth every penny. Not only that but you can host multiple websites off of one host account.

If you are planning on purchasing through Bluehost, I would be eternally grateful if you use my affiliate link: Bluehost.

iPage:

I have also used iPage for about five different websites. I strayed from Bluehost for a while just to see what else was out there. While iPage is relatively inexpensive and their support is fantastic, there is one major flaw… The speed of the website. While my website isn't extremely slow, I won't say I am satisfied with the speed. The load time is horrendous at times, but it is still doable.

If you are planning on purchasing through iPage, I would once again be eternally grateful if you use my affiliate link: iPage.

Both of these hosts have a really easy to use control panel. This is important because it will allow you to quickly install WordPress on your website with the click of a mouse. You don't have to do a THING!

For inexperienced users I would recommend just purchasing your domain name through whichever web host you choose.

If you know what you are doing as far as changing nameservers are confused, or you aren't afraid of learning, you can purchase through GoDaddy. Once you have purchased both web hosting and a domain name, you will need to change the nameservers on your domain to match your hosting domain name.

Choosing a WordPress Theme

Think of a WordPress theme as your storefront. You could have the most amazing product in the world but if your storefront is deterring visitors, they'll never come in. I know, I know, there are always exceptions to this rule, but let's keep it on the majority.

Free Themes vs. Paid Themes

While there are numerous themes available on the market, it is important to understand the pros and cons of all.

Free themes are awesome for those people who may be on a tight budget. There are so many out there to choose from, but I must warn you, there are cons to a free theme. While you can customize your free theme to your heart's content, there may be hidden backlinks present. This means that the creator of the theme is receiving free links to his or her website just because you are using it. On top of that, the support and updates for you free theme may be non-existent. If you have any trouble with it, you may not be able to find someone to help. On top of that, if it isn't kept up to date, it could lead to holes in your security.

Paid themes, while some are expensive, are the way to go if you have some money for it in your budget. There are many different companies out there that produce themes regularly, and their support is outstanding. Within hours you can have the answer to a question that has been driving you crazy. The customization options with a paid theme typically are much broader and you have a lot more control. If you go with a trusted source, you won't have to worry about hidden links on your website. On top of all that, the browser and mobile compatibility with paid themes should be enough to sway you.

Using A Relevant Theme

Choosing a theme relevant to your niche is something you may want to consider. For instance, if I was blogging about photography, it would be silly to have a theme related to cooking, and vice-versa.

A lot of the best themes can be adapted and customized to fit any niche, but not all. So, when choosing a theme, if you can find one that suits your industry, I highly recommend you take it. If not, choose a theme that can be customized almost any way you'd like.

Mobile and Browser Compatibility are Key

Any theme worth using will include details on browser and mobile compatibility. According to W3Counter.com, the **six** most popular web browsers that people use are:

1) Google Chrome
2) Safari
3) Mozilla Firefox
4) Internet Explorer
5) Android
6) Opera

You do not want to lose viewers because your theme doesn't support their browser! Note, Safari and Android are both mobile/tablet based browsers. That is a large percentage of your viewership!

Avoid Java and Flash like a Plague

Recommendations
How to Install a Theme

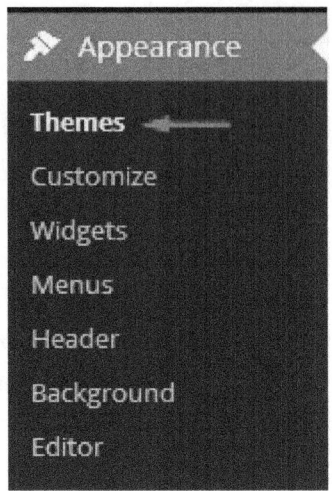

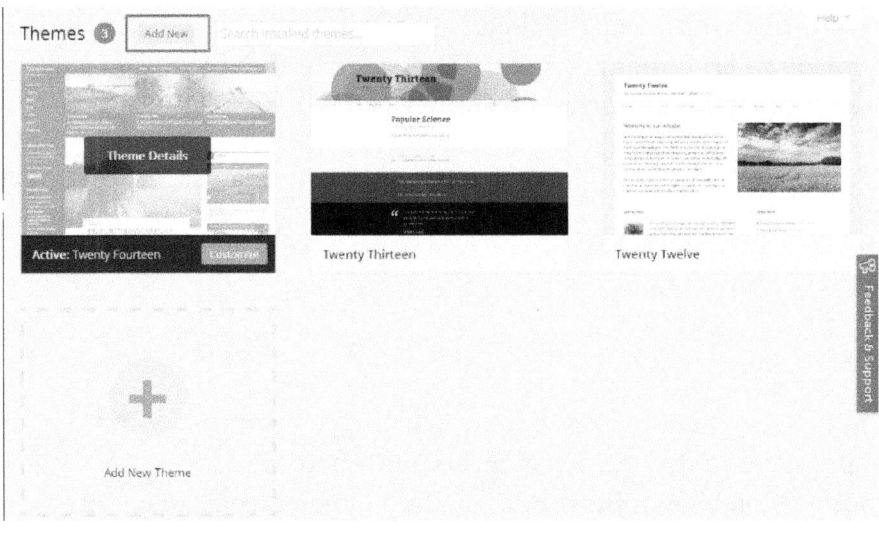

Add Themes Browse

If you have a theme in a .zip format, you may install it by uploading it here.

Choose File Divi.zip   Install Now

Installing Theme from uploaded file: Divi.zip

Unpacking the package...

Installing the theme...

Theme installed successfully.

Live Preview | Activate | Return to Themes page

Securing your Blog

So, it all started probably 2 years ago... I had just created my first blog and I was feeling good. I did no research whatsoever and I literally was just guessing at everything, including website security. In other words, I had no security.

My blog had been up for three weeks when I realized it started to slow down. I received an email from one of my users warning me there was Malware on my website, but meh, I really couldn't be bothered with something so small at that time. My main goal was just to generate content as fast as possible.

Then came the login warnings, telling me that another user had been logged into my account from Germany. Me, being half German, thought maybe it was just some long lost relative that saw my last name and decided to help out... (not really, I just didn't know what to do)

Proceed to about 2 weeks after all this started happening, I visited my website, but it was no longer my website. My once was blog was forwarded to some sort of German porno website or something. It was quite strange, but I learned my lesson.

After I talked to my webhost, they helped get my blog back up, but unfortunately I had to redo almost all of my most recent content. It was an error that I would never make again. I did my research and figured out exactly what precautions to take in order to prevent any such security breach from reoccurring.

Blog security in today's world is changing constantly. As your blog grows, you will be under the scope of many different hackers, so take the proper precautions. I have thirteen tips for securing your blog that everyone should put into play.

1) **Ensure your passwords are strong, and change them as often as possible.**

I know, this is the biggest pain in the butt ever, but I promise it will save you in the long run. Initially, I was resistant to frequent changes in my passwords and I struggled to come up with something I could remember. Turns out not remembering your password comes with the territory and it actually makes it stronger. Think about it, if you could remember your password, chances are there is someone out there who can crack it.

My suggestion is quite simple, build yourself an excel spreadsheet with all your admin logins (I highly recommend 3 admin accounts, as you will see in just a moment), and use a random password generator weekly or twice a week.

Easy tool to use: http://passwordsgenerator.net/

Secure Password Generator — makeuseof

Password Length:	15
Include Symbols:	(e.g. @#$)
Include Lowercase Letters:	✔ (e.g. abcdefg)
Include Uppercase Letters:	✔ (e.g. ABCDEFG)
Include Numbers:	✔ (e.g. 1234567890)
Exclude Similar Characters:	✔ (e.g. i, l, o, 1, 0, I)
Generate On The Client:	✔ (create the password locally, it will NOT be sent across the Internet)
Save My Preference:	✔ (save the above settings in client cookies)

Generate secure password

	A	B	C
1	**Camping Site Admin Passwords**		
2	**Username**	**Password**	**Last Updated**
3	admin333	nEALzv4vA7fzAps	15-Mar-14
4	admin292	ysThEAUC7GTBnkh	15-Mar-14
5	ultimateadmin	vgGYJfg2XYZjGnG	15-Mar-14

2) Use different passwords for every part of your blog.

Believe it or not, this simple tactic can prevent even the smartest of hackers from accessing your blog. What do I mean by this?

It's simple, you will typically have three different passwords for your blog.

1) The first password is to your webhosting.
2) The second password is to your FTP.
3) The third passwords are to your admin accounts on your blog.

Do your due diligence and ensure that all three of these passwords differ. You do not need to constantly change the first two, but you can if you want to take even further precautions.

3) Back up your blog weekly, and after any important changes.

One of the biggest lifesavers for you will be a WordPress automatic backup plugin. It will automatically save your website so you can restore it at a given point.

There are several plugin options out there, some free, some paid, but my favorite is BackWPup. It is free and really easy to use. I will show you my settings below:

Please name this job.	Default

Job Tasks

This job is a ...
- ☑ Database backup
- ☑ File backup
- ☑ WordPress XML export
- ☑ Installed plugins list
- ☐ Check database tables

Backup File Creation

Archive name

backwpup_3ab3e5_%Y-%m-%d_%H-%i-%s

Preview: backwpup_3ab3e5_2014-06-10_21-26-16.tar.gz

Archive Format
- ⦿ Zip
- ○ Tar
- ○ Tar GZip
- ○ Tar BZip2

Job Destination

Where should your backup file be stored?
- ☐ Backup to Folder
- ☑ Backup sent via email
- ☐ Backup to FTP
- ☐ Backup to Dropbox
- ☐ Backup to an S3 Service v1
- Backup to Microsoft Azure (Blob)
  PHP Version 5.2.17 is to low, you need Version 5.3.2 or above.
- Backup to Rackspace Cloud Files
  PHP Version 5.2.17 is to low, you need Version 5.3.3 or above.
- ☐ Backup to SugarSync

Job Schedule

Start job
- manually only
- ● with WordPress cron
- with a link ▓▓▓▓▓▓▓▓▓▓▓▓▓▓▓▓▓▓▓

Start job with CLI   Use WP-CLI to run jobs from commandline or get the start script.

Schedule execution time

Next runtime: Mon, 16 Jun 2014, 03:00

Scheduler type
- ● basic
- advanced

Scheduler

Type			Hour	Minute
monthly	on 1. ▾		3 ▾	0 ▾
● weekly	Monday ▾		3 ▾	0 ▾
daily			3 ▾	0 ▾
hourly				0 ▾

You can mess around with the different settings, but those are the settings I use.

4) Do NOT use cracked plugins, and research each new plugin to ensure its security.

I know, it is quite tempting to avoid paying for plugins. Using torrenting websites in order to acquire things for free is something almost everyone has done. I highly suggest that you DO NOT do this when it comes to WordPress plugins.

It's quite easy for the torrent to have been infected with malware, spyware, or anything of that sort. You put your website at risk by installing a bugged program, and it's just not worth it in the long run. If you are really dying to have a plugin that costs money, pay the few bucks and get it.

Also, research new plugins to see their legitimacy. Someone could have just uploaded a plugin which contains a virus. You do not want to be the sucker that gets caught with this. I would suggest googling the plugin and reading some reviews and what others are saying.

5) Create multiple admin accounts.

As I mentioned above, creating multiple admin accounts with different usernames can be beneficial. If one of your admin accounts were to get hijacked, it would be ideal to have another account to login with.

♻ 4   💬 15   **+ New**   SEO   🚫 BackWPup

Post
Media
Page
User

Add New Use

Create a brand new u   te.

Username *(required)*

E-mail *(required)*

First Name

Last Name

Website

Password *(required)*

Repeat Password *(required)*

Strength indicator   *Hint: The password sho*

Send Password?   ☐ Send this password to the new user by email.

Role   Administrator ▼

Add New User

To create a new administrator account just click "New" at the top, then "User." After, fill in the form, select the administration role and you're good to go!

6) Removing WordPress version text.

This is rather easy to do and worth the few seconds it takes to do it. WordPress will display on your site which version is running. You want to remove this so hackers do not know which exploits are available to use. This may deter them from ever trying to hack your website and is just one more tool in your tool belt.

To do this, hover over "Appearance" on the left and click "Editor."

Then, search for Functions.php (sometimes called Theme Functions).

Add in the following code:

remove_action('wp_head', 'wp_generator');

Click "Update File" and you're all set!

7) Keeping your plugins and themes up to date.

This is critical to your safety, and although it can be a pain in the butt, PLEASE make sure you always keep things up to date.

A lot of themes/plugins will patch vulnerabilities in security and require a quick update.

To do this it is quite simple, on the left of your WordPress admin panel you will see "Dashboard," click it and then click "Updates."

Select all, click "Update" and wait a few minutes (it's that easy)!

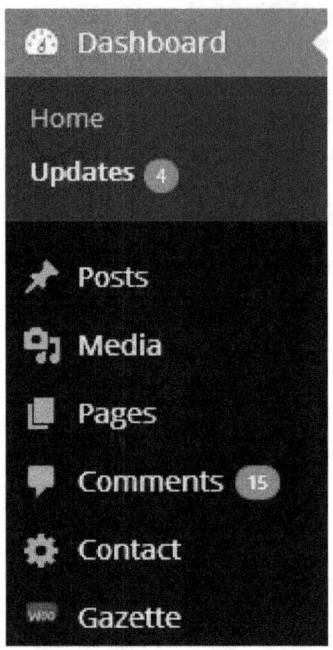

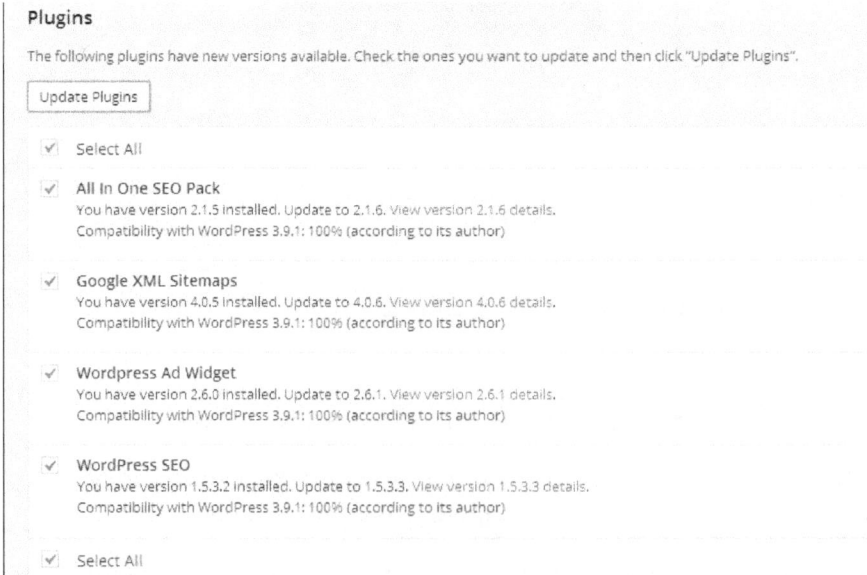

Plugins

The following plugins have new versions available. Check the ones you want to update and then click "Update Plugins".

Update Plugins

☑ Select All

☑ All In One SEO Pack
You have version 2.1.5 installed. Update to 2.1.6. View version 2.1.6 details.
Compatibility with WordPress 3.9.1: 100% (according to its author)

☑ Google XML Sitemaps
You have version 4.0.5 installed. Update to 4.0.6. View version 4.0.6 details.
Compatibility with WordPress 3.9.1: 100% (according to its author)

☑ Wordpress Ad Widget
You have version 2.6.0 installed. Update to 2.6.1. View version 2.6.1 details.
Compatibility with WordPress 3.9.1: 100% (according to its author)

☑ WordPress SEO
You have version 1.5.3.2 installed. Update to 1.5.3.3. View version 1.5.3.3 details.
Compatibility with WordPress 3.9.1: 100% (according to its author)

☑ Select All

8) Delete any unused themes or plugins.

Deleting themes and plugins that are not being used seems like it might be pointless, but it is not. Having unneeded themes and plugins can create unnecessary backdoors to your website that can easily be prevented. Just simply delete all the plugins and themes you are not using, and you have already solved a security risk!

Note: I recommend uninstalling a plugin every time you deactivate it do not plan to use it again. This will save you from having to delete 10 plugins at once, and keeping up on it is quite easy.

9) Use Pingdom to check your blog's downtime.

Pingdom is typically a paid service, but they offer a very useful free service which you should take full advantage of. It is a simple service where you can input your website and you'll receive an email any time it goes down.

http://www.pingdom.com/free

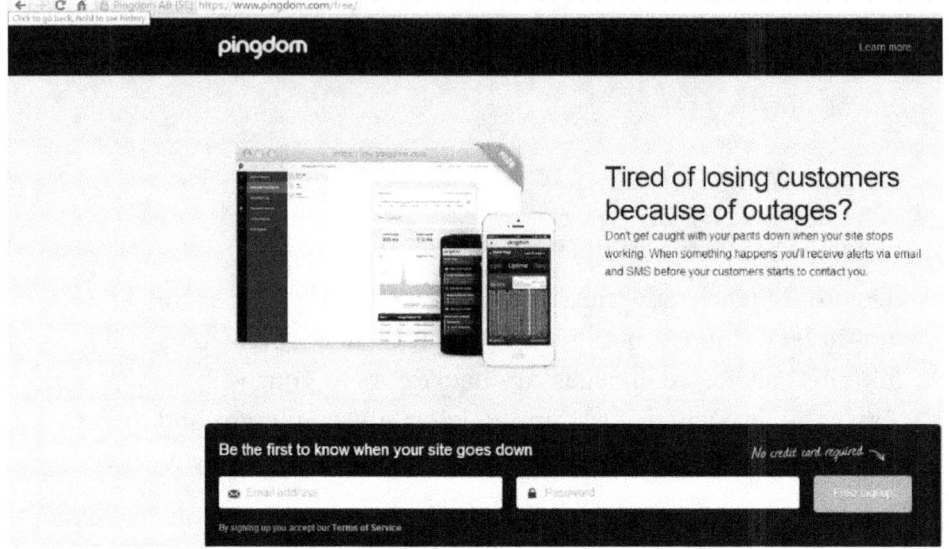

10) Sucuri's free scan will save you a headache.

If you want to quickly scan to see if you have any malware on your website or if you are blacklisted from any search engines, Sucuri is the website for you.

It is free and will tell you within minutes if you have anything to be concerned about on your website.

Head over to: https://sucuri.net/ input your website, and click "scan this site."

Warning: This could take a few minutes, be patient!

Free Website Malware and Security Scanner

| SiteCheck Results | Website Details | Blacklist Status |

Website: www.testing.com
Status: No Malware Detected by External Scan. Additional Actions Recommended!
Web Trust: Not Currently Blacklisted (8 Blacklists Checked)

Scan	Result	Severity	Recommendation
Malware	Not Detected	Low Risk	
Website Blacklisting	Not Detected	Low Risk	
Injected SPAM	Not Detected	Low Risk	
Defacements	Not Detected	Low Risk	
Website Firewall	Not Found	Medium Risk	PATCH AND PROTECT With Sucuri Firewall

They will try to sell you on a firewall, do not buy it, I have another solution in the next step!

11) Installing a firewall to prevent hackers.

As promised, I am going to let you in on a little secret… Okay, it's not a secret, just another plugin that I recommend for your website's security. It's a nifty little firewall for free, and pairing it with the plugin in step #12, your website will be like the Titanic, impossible to sink (joking of course, more like Fort Knox).

The plugin is called Centrora Security. It is fairly easy to understand so I did not attach any screenshots this time.

12) Install a security plugin to your website, I prefer iThemes Security.

There are countless security plugins out there that you can try out, but my favorite has to be iThemes Security. It is really complex on the backend, but so easy to set up. It is exactly what I was looking for when I needed a security plugin.

I have been using it for 8 months, and I have had no problems as far as security breaches go.

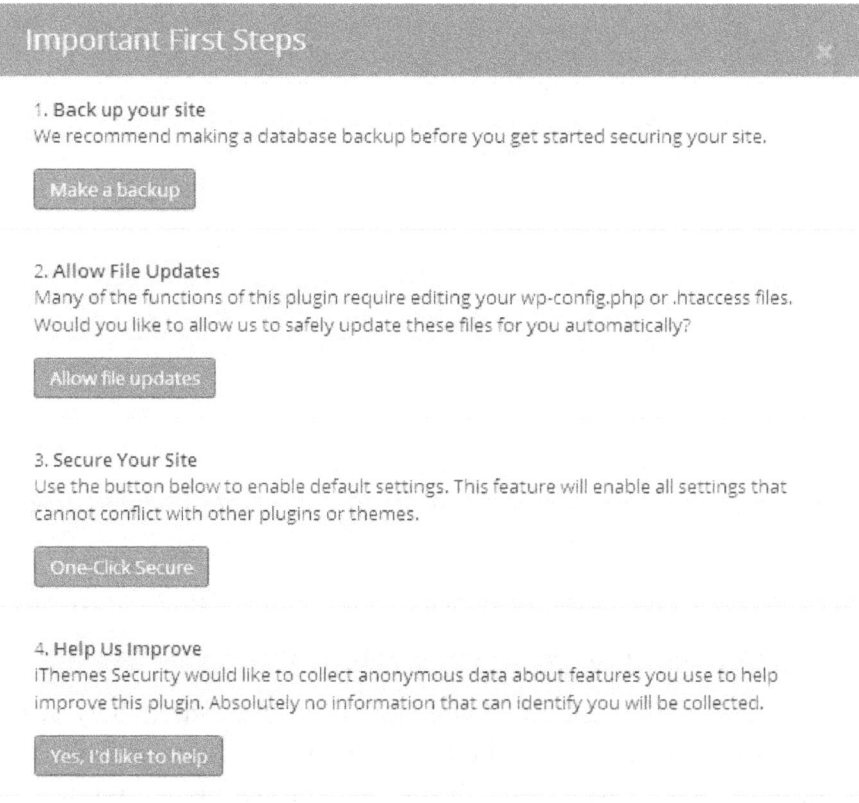

After installing, the box above will pop up when you navigate to the securities dashboard.

- Don't worry about backing up your site if you did in the previous steps.
- Allow the file updates.

- Click the "One-Click Secure" button.

One of the coolest things about iTheme Security is it will provide a list of actions one should take immediately to secure your website further. I recommend completing all of the "High Priority" and "Medium Priority" items in your dashboard. After you've completed all the required actions, move on to step 13.

13) Sign up for CloudFlare for free!

Head over to CloudFlare's Website and sign up for an account. You will be asked to enter your website, and taken through a few steps before reaching the following settings page.

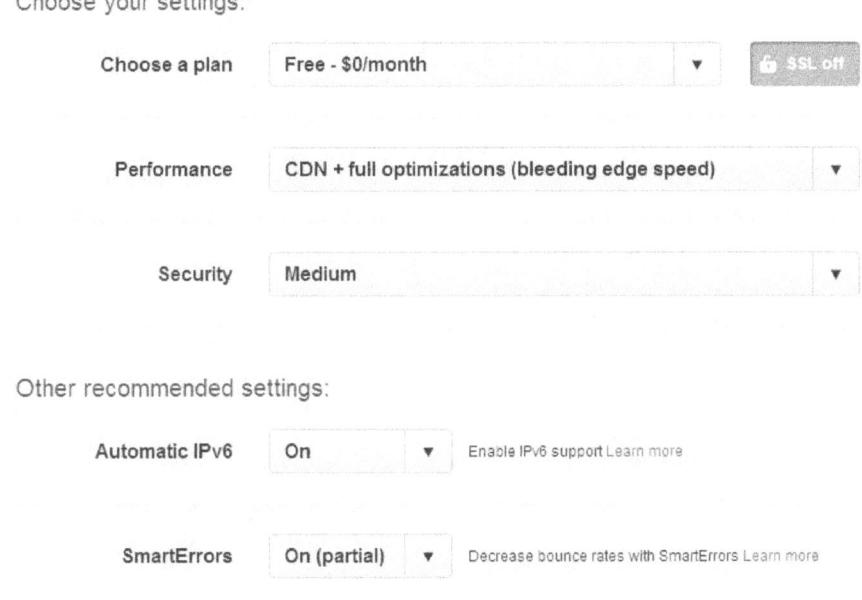

You can choose whichever settings you feel fit your website best, those are the ones which I prefer. You will then be asked to change your nameservers. You should be able to find the documentation on changing name servers through your domain host. Here are a few common guides:

- GoDaddy's Guide to Changing Nameservers

- Bluehost's Guide to Changing Nameservers
- iPage's Guide to Changing Nameservers

After you change your nameservers, click continue at the bottom of the CloudFlare page. You will then be asked to whitelist their IP address, which you may or may not need to do.

You are finished! You've not only increased your website's speed, but you've increased the security as well, remember: we're building Fort Knox here.

Optimize your Blog BEFORE Opening

There is nothing worse than trying to install plugins, add new posts, and change things up on a slower than slow website. I've been there, I've done that… Think about it, if you are annoyed by the speed of your site, just imagine your visitors!

We're in a day and age where websites have a near instant load time, and anything less is unacceptable and 'cheap.' You do not want to lose visitors before they're even able to load your beautiful infographic or detailed blog post, do you?

Don't worry, I have a simple six step solution (alliteration at its finest) to solving your issues.

1) **Only use the necessary plugins, I know it's tempting to download everything, but don't!**

Let's face it, there are tens of thousands of WordPress plugins that are available, but not all of them are needed. Some are luxuries, some cost money, some promise the world, but only a few are truly worth including in your blog. At the end of this book, I compiled a list of all the plugins I mentioned, and you shouldn't need much more than that.

Moral of the story: be very selective with your plugins. Do not choose them based on impulse, but rather on necessity. Whenever you stop using a plugin, uninstall it.

2) **Optimize images before uploading them.**

There are plugins that you can use to reduce the memory size of your images, but that would somewhat contradict the point I just made in step one. There is a simple piece of software you can install and use for your images that is very simple, it's called Shrink O' Matic and can be found here.

If you really must use a plugin, I would recommend downloading Smush.it.

Reducing the memory of an image can drastically increase the load speed of a given individual page, while not taking away from the quality.

3) Install a cache plugin.

A cache plugin will create a 'cookie' if you will for your returning visitors. Since they've already loaded the website once, it will load almost instantly upon their next visit.

The most popular plugin for caching is called W3 Total Cache; I highly recommend it!

4) Use a Content Delivery Network.

I mentioned a CDN in the previous section called CloudFlare. CloudFlare is not only used for security, but for optimizing your website as well.

What is a Content Delivery Network you ask?

In Layman's terms, a CDN will replicate your website on multiple servers around the world and connect your traffic to the closest possible server.

For instance, I live in Arizona and let's say I am connecting to a blog on a CDN. The website has been replicated in the following locations: California, New York, Chicago and Texas.

Since I am so close to California, I will automatically be routed to the California server. This will speed up my connection time to the server, and reduce the server load.

5) Reduce the clutter on your sidebar and website in general.

I know widgets can be fun, and having a sidebar with every widget you can find may be hard to resist, but please do. Removing a bunch of clutter from your side bar will not only speed up the load time on your website, it will make your website look a lot prettier. You do not want to overwhelm your visitors with too much information!

6) Stay away from java-based themes.

While java and flash themes may look great, they are not so great for optimization and definitely not SEO. The images and code takes computers a longer time to process and takes up a lot of memory. Not only that but Google will have a hard time crawling and indexing new pages on a java-based website. Simplicity is king.

Section III – Search Engine Optimization

Start with a good foundation of plugins

Before you even start posting, you can drastically increase your SEO efforts just by adding a couple of plugins. Although you cannot solely rely on these plugins for search engine ranking, they will give google the meet it needs to make your website appealing. I have compiled a list of plugins that I highly recommend you use, I also have provided alternatives just in case:

1) **WordPress SEO by Yoast**
    a. **All In One SEO Pack**
    b. **Scribe SEO**
    c. **SEO Presser**
    d. **SEO Ultimate**
2) **Google Libraries**
3) **Twitter Feed Pro**
    a. **The Official Twitter Widget**
    b. **Simple Twitter Tweets**
    c. **Recent Tweets Widget**
    d. **WP Twitter Feeds**
4) **Simple URLs**
    a. **SEO Smart Links**
    b. **SEO Auto Links**
5) **SEO Friendly Images**
    a. **Wordpress SEO For Image**

SEO Brings 'Em, Content Keeps 'Em

The plain and simple truth is if you don't have quality content, you're not going to acquire and retain quality readers. This all goes back to one of my initial points, have **passion** for what you're writing. If you don't have passion, you more than likely don't have the drive to finish an article. If you are forcing yourself to do something, then is it really your best work?

I have a story to share, although it is a little out there, you can somewhat relate it to this topic. As a child, I was always forced by my mother to go to church. Every Sunday it was the same fight, I would tell her I didn't want to go, she would drag me out of bed and force me to. Some Sundays I would fake being sick just to try and avoid going (it didn't ever work).

Finally, I turned 18, and guess what… I didn't have to go anymore! So what do you think I did? I didn't go. I honestly resented going to church for a long time after I turned 18.

The moral of the story is, forcing yourself to write about something you aren't interested in, is just going to push you away from that topic and blogging in general.

Have you ever been on a blog, read an article, and instantly realized how much you regret reading said article? I know I have. There are so many articles out there that have no voice; they almost feel as if they're written by a robot. How many readers do you think you will retain if your articles are dry and lacking in quality content? You may retain a few, but they are going to be unresponsive and useless, just like your articles (Ok, that was a bit harsh).

But let's get into the meat of this subject…

1) Choosing A Topic

I can't tell you exactly how your brain works, but I can tell you this: Most people have thoughts throughout the day, ideas, something to spark their creative mind, but a crucial mistake is often made… These ideas aren't written down.

If you ever have an idea pop into your head, pull out your phone, grab a piece of paper, write it in your journal, or if none of these things are possible say it 10 times quickly in your head. All these random ideas you have during the day are going to help make your blog unique and worth coming back to.

 ### Section III, Activity I

Let's say you post every other day or so. Open up your journal or wherever you're recording your ideas and scan for the top two or three ideas. Separate these ideas out and write down bullet points for each idea. Remember, you're more than likely trying to solve a problem or provide valuable information on the topic, so make sure there's enough to write about. After you've created bullet points for your ideas, one will usually jump out at you, so choose that.

Note: I would save your other topics because they can be useful for future posts

HealthFreakRecipes.com

Ideas
- Quick Breakfast Recipes
☆ - Top Super Foods
- Quinoa - A detailed Guide
- 15 minute Lunch Recipes
- Can Healthy Food Be Tasty?
☆ - Health Supplements On the Rise
- Healthy Recipes on A Budget

Top Super Foods	Health Supplements
- What are super foods?	- What are health supplements
- What makes them "super?"	- Are they actually beneficial
- Top 10 Super foods & Nutritional Info	- Top 5 Supplements & how to
- Super Supper Recipes	use them

Still stuck? Here are some ideas for coming up with a worth-while blogging topic:

- **Think About Your Audience:** When you sit down to write your post, put yourself in the head of your readers. Close your eyes, and become one of your readers. Think about what information you'd be wanting to read on your topic, think about what questions said reader may have, what information is out there already? What information is missing in the current market? How can you be different than everyone out there? If you can answer those questions, you will be able to create a quality blog post.
- **Something YOU Want To Write About:** Look, sometimes we just want to write what's on our mind. There is absolutely nothing wrong with that logic. If you have some burning desire to write on a specific topic, DO IT. No one is holding

you back, this is your blog; you have total creative control. Something that always happens to me is I'll be reading a book and come across some interesting topic. I take notes, do research, and then I go enlighten all my friends on the topic because I have a burning desire to teach the topic. After I've told all my friends about the topic, I put pen to paper and start crafting a blog post to share with my readers. After all, teaching others helps you retain information nearly 70% better than any other method.

- **One Topic Per Post:** I can't stress this enough, keep your topic one dimensional. You do not want to have three different topics crammed into one post, because it will get confusing to your readers. You will lose readers if you make your posts confusing and complex. I'm sure we've all heard the phrase: KISS, Keep It Simple Stupid. Not only will it increase your retention rate, but it will improve your visibility on search engines AND you can save the extra content for another unique post.

- **Trending Topics:** So you've gotten to this point and you still feel like you're stuck and really don't know what to do… Okay, well, it's time to pull out the big guns. Head over to www.Google.com/Trends and do some exploring. These are all the hot ticket search terms in real time. You can choose which category you're looking for and see exactly what people want this minute. The problem is most of these are fads, so you need to get on them as quickly as possible. I wouldn't write down a list of 20 and use it next month. These are topics that need a post within a day or two of seeing them trending.

- **Identify A Need In Your Niche:** So, the most obvious tip I can give you is to solve a problem. What I would do is pull up a few of your competitors' websites and see what they've written on recently. If you read through their websites and realize that there is a clear disconnect or hole in their content, write that down! It is the perfect way to solve a problem and fill a gap in the industry that might otherwise go unnoticed. You can even scan the comments and read the ongoing debates/criticisms of the article.

As you can see, coming up with a topic isn't rocket science. There are so many different methods to figure out what you'd want to write about. Be the catalyst in your market, be the change. Don't be redundant, don't copy other peoples' topics. Readers will come if your content is unique, so start with a unique topic.

2) Titling Your Blog Post

I know you've heard the saying, "A picture is worth a thousand words." Well, for blogging, *a title is worth a thousand readers.*

I'm not joking, a title is going to make or break an article… no pressure though.

Really, no pressure, because I'm going to give you some tips that will make your title the best it possibly can be.

1) Don't title your post before you have finished writing it. Your title should be the last piece of your article because it needs to be relevant. Maybe you went off on a tangent in your post, and it completely changed the context. If you already had a title, guess what? You have to come up with a new one now.

2) Keep it simple. But Jordan, you already said that… Yeah, I did just mention keeping it simple in the topic above, but I want to stress the importance of keeping a title simple. Research has proven time and time again that shorter sells. There is a reason why the Apple App Store only allows 35 character titles. You don't want to reveal your entire secret in your title, you just want enough to grab their attention.

3) Grabbing your reader's attention. A great title will captivate the reader before they've even read a sentence.

There are numerous tactics for grabbing someone's attention: controversy, confusion, mystery, a big claim, or even shock factor. But be really careful using these tactics, you need to ensure that your post lives up to your promise. Your title, after all, is the promise and premise of your post.

4) Keywords are king. You've done your keyword research for your topic and decided on two or three you really want to target. Don't be shy, use one of these in your title. If you use this tactic, you can easily build the rest of your title around the keyword. It adds direction and improves search engine visibility.

5) Time, time time. Look, you have all the time in the world to come up with a quality title. There is NO rush. Write down 15 title ideas, flesh them out, conduct research on some quality headlines that others have used, use whatever tactic you have to. Lacking a quality title is like drawing a beautiful picture with chalk and then it starts to rain… goodbye picture.

 Section III, Activity II

It's time to get hands on again. Pop open google and search for something related to your topic. From there, have a look at all the titles being used by your competitors, and circle some words you like. Write these words down and come up with a good title from just these words.

For instance, I searched "super foods" to coincide with my previous activity, here are the results:

News for **super foods**

12 **Superfoods** You Should Know About
NDTV - 6 days ago
Here's a checklist of the healthiest **super foods** and why they are good for you.

Superfoods could actually be bad for your health
Toronto Star - 6 days ago

Shoppers could save £440 a year swapping wheatgrass for ...
The Guardian - 1 day ago

More news for **super foods**

Dr. Perricone's 10 **Superfoods** - Oprah.com
www.oprah.com/health/Dr-Perricones-10-**Superfoods** ▾ Oprah Winfrey ▾
Learn Dr. Perricone's 10 **superfoods** and how they make the beauty-brain connection. They're rich in the Essential Fatty Acids (EGAs), antioxidenants, fiber or all ...

Diabetes **Superfoods**: American Diabetes Association®
www.diabetes.org/food.../food/...food.../d... ▾ American Diabetes Association ▾
There isn't research that clearly points to supplementation, so always think first about getting your nutrients from foods. Below is our list of **superfoods** to include ...

In-depth articles

Tim Ferriss: 10 Uncommon '**Superfoods**' From the ...
The Huffington Post - May 2013
"We've all heard of acai, goji berries and chia seeds. But I'd be willing to bet most of you are unfamiliar with more than a few of these more obscure **superfoods**."

Explore: tim ferriss diet

Healthy Superfood Grains - Freekeh, Farro ...
Oprah Winfrey - Apr 2011
4 Exotic Grains That Can Improve Your Health. These ancient **superfoods** from all corners of the world are worth rediscovering. By Leslie Goldman. 1 of 4. Freekeh. Photo: Levi Brown ...

Explore: grains

Pomegranate Supreme Court case: **Food** industry ...
Slate - May 2014
The food industry's devious, ingenious, magical misuse of science. .... Not with food or pills, of course, but rather a healthy dose of skepticism about claims that certain 'super' foods do ...

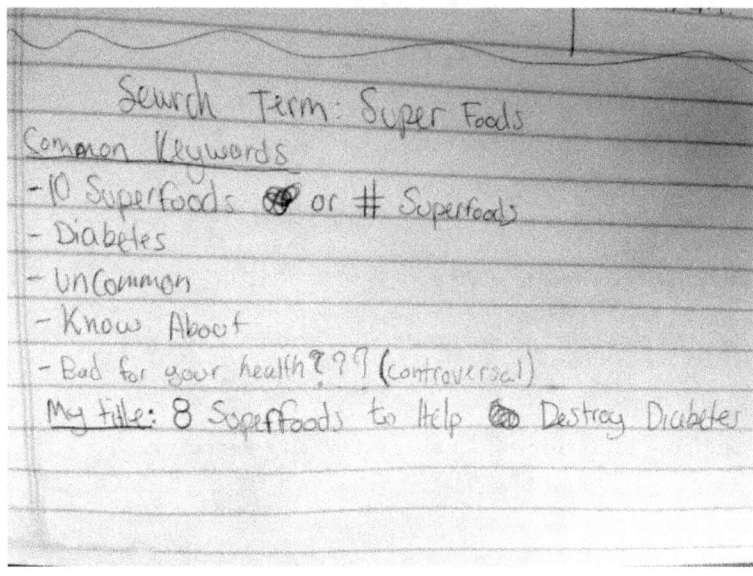

I grabbed bits and pieces from each of the articles and wrote them down. After, I was able to craft a decent title with an alliteration as well. Not only do you want your title to describe, but you want it to draw the attention of your readers. Using alliteration is a great way to peak the attention of potential readers (Destroy Diabetes). I also made a big claim in my article title. Obviously diabetes isn't reversible, but that doesn't mean it can't be combatted and reduced, which is what I'd plan on writing about in this article.

3) Formatting Your Post For Skimming

When I first get onto a webpage, I will scroll all the way down and look at the headings, pictures, bolded font, etc. If there is something that grabs my attention specifically, I will stop, and read whatever it is. Now, if the information provided under the heading that I read was valuable, I will scroll all the way back up and read the article from the start.

This is a common tactic used by many readers and it is important for us as writers to know. This is getting into the head of your audience and potential readers.

What can we do as writers to ensure these readers are captured as future returning consumers?

It's quite simple really, we need to do the following:

- Add lists into your blog. Bullet points and bold font will instantaneously gain the reader's attention.
- Formatting is a tool you need to harness and have full control over. Use font color changes, *italics*, **BOLD,** underlines, *a combination.* Just don't get too crazy with this or else it will lose its meaning.
- Headings and subheadings, as I mentioned previously, are a big part of your article. These should take some time to come up with and really draw the reader in. Remember in school how they told us our introductory sentence needed to draw the attention of readers? Think of these headings as your intro sentence.
- Pictures, pictures, pictures. There are so many different types of learners out there, but research shows that nearly everyone is drawn in by pictures. Use them to your advantage, but don't over use them or misplace them. These pictures need to captivate and tell a story. Putting a picture of a dog on a recipe article probably won't convey the proper message. Make sure they pertain to your topic and are relevant to the section you use them in.
- Separate your quotes by adding boxes. If that sounds foreign to you, here's what I mean:

Before my current examples, let's look at a basic template from The 4-Hour Workweek. Readers have tested this one in 30+ languages:

> Greetings, Friends [or Esteemed Colleagues],
>
> Due to high workload, I am currently checking and responding to e-mail twice daily at 12: 00 P.M. ET [or your time zone] and 4: 00 P.M. ET.
>
> If you require urgent assistance (please ensure it is urgent) that cannot wait until either 12: 00 P.M. or 4: 00 P.M., please contact me via phone at 555-555-5555.
>
> Thank you for understanding this move to more efficiency and effectiveness. It helps me accomplish more to serve you better.
>
> Sincerely,
>
> [Your name]

(Credit: www.fourhourworkweek.com)

As you can see, Tim Ferriss uses the tactic I was just describing effectively. He wanted to draw the attention of his readers to one specific area, and he does so by indenting and adding a grey box.

- Finally, proper spacing creates an easy-to-read article and increases your read through rate drastically. No one wants to read a wall of text, it is intimidating. This isn't academic writing, no teacher is going to mark off for improper spacing and too short of paragraphs. Use the "return" key to your advantage!

4) Adding In A CTA (Call To Action)

What do you want your reader to do?

Do you want your reader to join on the discussion? Subscribe? Buy something? Share your article?

I'll ask again, what do you want your reader to do?

It may be a really simple question that you can easily answer, but just make sure you can. If you can't answer this question, your reader can't answer this question. Maybe you're just providing information to your reader, but passive readers are the worst kind.

You want your reader to take action, get involved, add value, whatever it may be.

- If you want your reader to answer a question, tell them to comment about it below.
- If you want your reader to subscribe to your email list, tell them how to do so and what they get for doing it.
- If you want them to share your article with their friends – ask!

You see where this is going.

This is what we in the internet marketing world call a "Call To Action" or CTA.

Read the following list to get a better understanding of what a CTA is and how to properly use one in a blog post:

1) Know your audience and what they're willing to do. For instance, if I was writing to an audience for my site: www.HealthFreakRecipes.com, I can expect that my audience loves to cook. An easy call to action for this particular group would be to go try out a new recipe and post their results in the comment section below. This makes my website fun and interactive. They will more than likely provide tips, criticisms, feedback, and valuable information for other readers. This is FREE content to your blog that you didn't have to write, capitalize on it!

2) Use one call to action each post, no more, no less. You don't want to overwhelm your readers with five different call to actions pointing them in every direction. Identify which call to actions would work best for which posts. If I know that I gain new readers through ten popular posts, it may be a good idea to make the call to action in those ten posts to subscribe to my email list (which I will be talking about later in this book).

3) Give your readers incentives for participating or acting on your CTA. If you are trying to get someone to subscribe

to your email list, tell them what they get for doing so. For instance, I would tell potential subscriber they will not be spammed, but they will receive a recipe book with ten delicious and healthy lunch recipes for subscribing. Let them know their benefits upfront, and then deliver on said benefits.

4) Here it comes again... KEEP IT SIMPLE, STUPID! I'm joking, you aren't stupid; you bought this product didn't you? What I mean is keep your call to action as generic and easy to do as possible. The challenge of the action can increase if you realize you have readers that respond well, but more likely than not, this isn't the case. For example, if I want to increase the number of comments on my post, I could run a contest that required users to comment on my post in order to be entered into a raffle. The comment could be something as simple as an opinion. Don't put too many limits on it, or else it will reduce the number of people who participate.

5) Mix it up! No one wants to hear the same call to action over, and over, and over. It gets repetitive and is a great way to lose readers. There are so many different actions you could have a reader take within your post, so let's do a quick brainstorming activity:

Section III, Activity III

Pretend you own a blog on the best restaurants in town. Think of three different call to actions you could implement into your posts, and write them down.

Call to Actions for Health Freak Recipes

1. Subscribe to my email list below and receive a Cookbook on the 10 Most delicious and Healthy Summer Lunch Recipes.

    [insert cover here]

2. What are you waiting for? Go try the recipe and come back to post your pictures and ~~some~~ opinion!

3. Want a $25 gift card to Bed Bath & Beyond? ~~Comment~~ Leave your opinion in a comment below and you'll automatically be entered into a raffle.

5) Separate Yourself From The Pack

You don't want your blog to be identical to your competitors, you need to dare to be different.

What is going to separate you from the fifteen other blogs on cooking?

- **Your content.** First and foremost, your content needs to be unique and fill holes that other posts don't. Go analyze your competitors' posts and figure out exactly what holes are in their post. Write an article that just fills the gap left by said bloggers, and trust me, there's always a gap.
- **Your tone and voice.** Be funny, be witty, be serious, provide insight, be a conversationalist. Since when did blogging have to be stuffy academic writing? I like to write as if I was speaking to someone. It allows the reader to create a dialog in their head and makes it feel as if you're in the room talking to them.

- **Take someone's content and add on to it.** If you just read an article that was talking about the Top 10 Restaurants in the Los Angeles area, and you disagree, create your own. Take a few from them that you agree with, but change it up, maybe make it the Top 10 Seafood Restaurants in the Los Angeles area.

6) Polish Before Publish

I can't stress this enough. Don't let your readers catch your careless grammatical and spelling mistakes. Give your article a thorough read through before hitting that elusive publish button. Find a friend, have said friend edit your article or skim it for mistakes. Pay an editor (if you can afford one) to correct any and all mistakes. You don't want your article to be stuffy, but you still want it to be professional.

7) Types Of Blog Posts

- o **Link posts:** Link posts are posts with a compilation of links. If you were writing a post on what items you need in a kitchen to be a successful chef, you could provide links to other articles, products, and resources in your article. You want to still include text, but these types of posts would be mainly linking out to other sites or products.
- o **Reviews:** Maybe you just got an awesome new knife called the Ninja 5000 (nerdy Harry Potter reference, sorry) and you absolutely love it. You take a picture and video of it in action, add it to your blog, add some content. Throw the word "review" in the title and provide your feedback for the different functions of a knife. This is sure to get you some views, heck I would even provide an affiliate link to the knife on Amazon so others can purchase it too!
- o **Lists:** These are some of the most common posts now-a-days, and if you're anything like me they draw

my attention in a heartbeat on my down time. These posts are the ones that you'll commonly see on BuzzFeed, "Top 10 Soccer Players of All Time." In the post they'll provide a picture and description of these soccer players. You can apply this method to your blog for easy/fun posts, but don't make your blog JUST list posts.

- **How To/Instructional:** These posts are the ones you'll see most frequently on websites like eHow. They are posts that provide a step-by-step guide to completing a certain action. If I wanted to teach people how to properly chop an onion, I could provide detailed typing with pictures, or provide a video with a voice over of me actually doing the chopping.
- **Interviews:** Interviews are a great way to add a different voice on your website and provide some credibility. If you're writing a blog post about becoming an expert cook, it would be really great to find someone who already has made a name for him or herself. If you could get them to do an extensive interview with you, you could post this in text or video format.
- **Rant posts:** I rant ALL the time. Ranting is awesome, fun, and funny; although don't do this too often. Sometimes I come across an issue I feel very strongly about. It may not even pertain to my blog, but I'll share it anyway. This is a highly opinionated and fiery post. Used properly, this can encourage a lot of discussion and controversy, just be careful not to scare off your readers!
- **Research:** I have a degree in Biology, and I'll tell you, the amount of research I did is unheard of. Research is a fantastic way to draw the skeptics in. If you decided that you were going to do a research

project on the outcome of baking chicken on different surfaces, you could easily document and make a blog post on said topic. Provide a lot of pictures, statistics, figures, and keep it academic.

o **Infographic:** Infographics hit the market not too long ago, and they blew up. It seemed everyone had to have an infographic for whatever their topic was. These are great for viral marketing. If you have a topic that you think could be explained in an infographic, I would say get it done!

The above are just a few examples of what you could be writing posts about. There are so many different and effective ways to structure your blog posts. I recommend using a bunch of different methods to not only keep your readers interested, but to ensure you don't get burned out of writing.

8) Frequently Asked Questions – Must Read

1) How long should my blog post be?

There is no specific length for your post, although I would suggest it being longer than 500 words. Search engines will look at your post to ensure it is natural, and the length certainly comes into play. Remember to stay on topic, you don't want to stray.

2) How often should I be adding new content to my blog?

Adding new content is an art. You don't want to overwhelm your readers with too much content, but you want enough on your website to keep them coming back. At the same time, you cannot burn yourself out. If you write too many articles, you will easily get burned out. I would say **2-3** quality articles a week should be your aim.

3) How do I optimize my blog post for search engine visibility?

The best way you can optimize your blog for SEO is picking one to three keywords per post and using them just enough. The Yoast SEO plugin will be your best friend as far as this goes. It provides feedback on exactly what you need to add or remove from your post to make it look natural and rank better on google.

4) What can I do if I get tired of posting or have to go on vacation?

This is quite simple really. First, if you get tired of posting, outsource it. There are so many different outlets to purchase articles from for low prices. If you need to take some time off, go drop $100 and get 5-7 articles. Second, if you are going on vacation, create your content (or purchase it) ahead of time. Add your content onto WordPress and you can set the date and time on the right hand side on when the post should be published. WordPress will automatically publish your post at the selected date, and you're good to go!

Launch Day! – Get it right

Creating Your Sales Pitch

A sales pitch is a critical part of any and every business. This is the first overall impression of your website, and it will ultimately determine if you're going to draw a reader in or be just another website.

The "sales pitch" for a blog is not a sales pitch at all; it is a tagline/slogan. The tagline should provide insight on what your blog is, but be entertaining as well. It is truly an art to come up with a quality tagline.

I find myself frequently using www.fiverr.com to come up with taglines. I just pay someone $5 to create 5 taglines for me. I will sift through the taglines, tweak them a bit, and BOOM, I'm ready to open.

Having multiple posts on launch day

While it is vital to have that one piece you are pushing above all else, it is also important to keep the readers interested after that post. If you want to gain subscribers and build a following, then have multiple pieces of content for them to consume.

I launched my camping website a long time ago with only one piece. I distinctly remember the article, it was *The Top 10 Camping Tents for the Summer Season*. It provided value and good content, but it just wasn't enough to captivate the readers to subscribe. I remember this being one of my biggest let downs.

I received numerous comments that suggested my post was great, but that was the problem, it was simply just **a** post, not plural.

Quite simply put, diversify right from the start. Make sure you have at least 4-5 posts that are of the highest quality. Think of these posts as the first time you introduced yourself to your significant other's parents. They leave impressions that will last a lifetime and dictate whether you retain readers or have to start all over again.

Hit Every Angle

In the previous chapter, I spoke about the different types of blog posts that exist. One important note about people is they respond differently to different kinds of posts. No one learns or is entertained the same, so keep this in mind for launch day.

If you know exactly what you want your viral post to be, that's great because it is really important, but your other pieces matter too.

I would choose 4-5 different types of blog posts for your blog before you launch. Make sure you appeal to the skeptics, the consumers, the right brained and the left brained. You want them to know you're here to cater to everyone and they should stick around.

For your viral piece, I recommend getting an interview with an expert, getting an expert to guest post, or even an infographic. You want to provide a fresh outlook or a completely new look on a specific topic. A piece going viral means people can't help but share it, so think to yourself, what can I do to separate myself from others and leave a lasting impression?

Google Alert

Head over to www.Google.com/alerts and set up some keywords for your website and for your name. This is a great way to find new trending topics to write about, but more importantly to see who is mentioning your website and/or your name.

This provides you the opportunity to connect with other individuals who mention you and thank them for doing so. It is just one more way to improve your public relations and get your name out there. Take advantage of it.

Build Relationships Before You Launch

There are many different forums, blogs, and communities out there which pertain to the blog topic you will be writing about. Whatever it may be, create a list of all of these and start building connections. Remember, the connections don't have to be with the owners of the communities, you can build relationships with the individuals using them as well. Once relationships are established, you can easily gain new readers by leveraging these connections. This is an awesome tactic to use on launch day.

Keyword Selection

Even if you have the greatest blog in the world, it might be difficult for people to find in search engines. That is, unless you take advantage of proper keyword use. If people type "awesome puppy stories" into their search engine, and your blog about puppy stories shows up, you are probably doing something right.

If you are new to the idea of using keywords for your blog, the concept is probably a little daunting. The first thing to learn is that "keywords" do not need to be single words at all. While they can be just one, they are often two or so words.

How often do you use a search engine to look for a single word? If you type "keywords" into Google, you're not likely to find what you really want. That is because single-word keywords are too "broad", meaning that they are not specific enough.

Using Google Insights

To find out what keywords you should focus on with your blog, there are some great tools out there. Luckily, Google provides one of these services to their users. With this tool, you can look at just how popular certain keywords are with users.

Finding Uncompetitive Keywords

Another important factor is how competitive keywords are. If there are already 500 popular blogs taking advantage of that "awesome puppy stories" keyword, and you are trying to break into that niche — you might want to focus on a variation of the keyword. Examples could be "coolest puppy stories", or "funny stories about puppies". It is also helpful to add slight variations of your best keywords.

How to Use Keywords

Okay, so you have a list of keywords that lots of users search for every day, but not too many people are already using for their own websites. It might seem like a great idea to just plaster those keywords all over your blog, right? Wrong. Search engines dislike sites that try to get the top spots on searches, without offering any good content.

You never know when Google is going to change their algorithms, and punish some methods for using keywords. That is why you should use your keywords naturally, and not too often.

Quality Images Are Required

You blog needs quality images for a number of reasons. They can help to explain things to your viewers, break up the text on your blog, and make your social media shares stand out with thumbnail images. Some people will even share a post with their friends, just because they liked an image that was used.

If you are not using *great* images on your blog — you are decreasing your chances of it ever becoming popular.

Taking Pictures from Other Sites

It is all too common for people to just "steal" images from other websites, and re-use them on their own blog. Laws regarded this type of thing are still being ironed out in the courts, but you can bet on one thing — your blog will not stand out if you use use other people's images.

Where to Find Cheap, Legal Images

You might not be the world's greatest artist, or any good at taking photographs, but you can still have quality images on your site. There are plenty of places that will sell you the rights to good images, for a very reasonable fee. While other bloggers might also use these images, you can at least make sure that your blog is totally legal.

Buying Unique Images

This is probably the most expensive method, but it's also the most professional. If you can buy unique images from artists, graphic designers, or photographers — your blog is really going to shine. Another perk of paying people for images, is that you can ask for customized work that suits your posts perfectly.

Creating Your Own Images

You don't have to be a great artist to make your own images for blogging. There is a variety of free digital imaging software available. It will take you a little longer, while you learn how to use your choice of software — but the results will be unique, and will not cost you anything, apart from some time and effort.

SEO Traffic Techniques

SEO (Search Engine Optimization) is about more than just using a bunch of keywords, and you don't have to *buy* good placements on the search engines.

There is no guaranteed, magical trick to ranking well in the search engines, and that's why some SEO services charge big money. However, with these simple tips, you can improve you blog's visibility on the popular search engines, like Google.

Use Killer Titles

Are you using killer titles for your blog posts? If your new post about top celebrity fails has the title "What Are These Guys Doing?", you are doing things wrong. How about "Celebrity Fails That You Won't Believe". Think about your chosen keywords when you choose titles, and make sure your titles fully describe what people will find on your posts.

Tags and Descriptions

You don't have to let search engines use default descriptions (that is, a random bit of text) when it lists your posts. Write them yourself, using your keywords and making them appealing to people. You should use them in your tags too, for everything that you post or share. Spending a little extra time to properly complete these details will improve your SEO nicely.

Link Juice

Links are a huge factor in SEO, because search engines assume that a good blog will contain lots of links from other places. You should never pay for links from shady looking services, though, because it could hurt your SEO. Companies like Google are aware of these little tricks, and they punish people who use them. On your own posts, add links to other posts on your blog, especially if they're related. This will increase your views too!

Guest Blogging Tactics

Writing guest posts for other websites and blogs is a great way to increase traffic for your own blog. The goal here isn't to write any old junk, and then spam your own links. If you are going to guest blog, do it right, and make something great. If popular bloggers see that you contribute unique, helpful content to other people — you just might get requests from some prominent bloggers. This is a wonderful way to increase your popularity, plus you can share your own links.

Make Guest Blogs Posts Unique

Don't just rehash something that you've already posted about on your own blog. That's not only a bad tactic, but also bad manners. Give other bloggers something special, even if it means you're giving away your best ideas. It will be worthwhile in the long run, as your standing as a reliable guest blogger increases.

Create Follow-up Posts

If you are going to write a guest post about cooking the perfect Sunday roast, why not create a sister post about the perfect way to set a table for family lunch? When you link to your sister post, it won't seem spammy at all, and people are more likely to want to read both posts. The next thing you know — you will be gaining plenty of new traffic.

Social Media Frenzy

You might have never thought of it, but a social media frenzy has been in action for several years. Ever since the popularity of sites like MySpace and Facebook first took hold of the world, the way that people have interacted with each other has never been the same.

Knowing about the social media frenzy is one thing, but how can you take advantage of it?

Use Popular Sources

Instead of trying to create a whole new place for people to gather and interact, why not go to them? If you really want to draw attention to your blog, make proper use of your own social media accounts. There are already plenty of people using those sites, so it's now easier than ever for smart people to make the most of it.

Create a Stir

Instead of using social media to talk at people about your blog, why not create interactions that people want to become involved in? Even if you post something that's controversial, it could become viral. In fact, controversy is a great way to get people's attention; just be careful not to give yourself a bad name in the process.

Understand the Frenzy

Social media is huge, but it's not guaranteed to help your blog. When a platform is that popular, there are already countless people trying to have their voices heard. You need to understand where you should place your efforts, instead of just plastering yourself everywhere.

Commenting On Blogs

Leaving comments on other blogs is a great way to get yourself out there, and also lead people back to your own posts. Of course, if you just go around posting links in the comment sections of your competition — people are going to assume that you're a spammer, and probably a bit of a jerk.

Add Value to Conversations

Leave comments that contribute to what other people are talking about, and interact with them in a meaningful way. You can also try to strike up your own conversations, and gain some followers and friends that way.

Demonstrate Your Expertise

If someone is trying to find an answer to a question, or they need a little help — it's a great opportunity to demonstrate how much you know about your niche. Don't give wrong advice though, or it might make you look like a fraud.

Be Nice!

The Internet is full of strong opinions, and arguments thrive. No matter what happens, you can't lose your cool. If someone annoys you, or even abuses you, the best thing to do is — be nice. Try to "kill them with kindness", or just disengage from talking to that person. It will make you seem like the bigger person, and you won't tarnish your reputation by coming off like a disagreeable person.

Using YouTube To Your Advantage

You probably already know it, but YouTube is insanely popular. Are you using that to help your own blog? Even if you are not a good video maker, there are ways that you can benefit from the popularity of YouTube.

Video is Fresh

Text content has been on the Internet since its creation. That means that most things have already been done — over and over. Widespread video content is still relatively new, as people around the world are getting faster connections, and enjoying the wonder of streaming videos. That means that you are more likely to create unique video content, compared to trying to write something new, or by using images.

You Need to Be Everywhere

If you really want to get your name out there, it's important to make use of every avenue. This includes video, and YouTube is probably the best way to do this.

Make Your Own Videos

Maybe being on camera scares the heck out of you, but you can still create the next viral video. Here are just some of the different types of videos you could create:

- Slideshow videos
- Screen Capture videos
- Text and audio videos
- Animations

The only limit here is your imagination, and what you are willing to learn to do.

Infographics Are The New Hot Ticket!

Using infographics is a great way to boost your views, and get people into discussions about your niche. There is so much information online, and there is way too much for any one person to read. Why not make it easier by using helpful infographics on your blog?

What Are They?

An infographic is an image that mixes graphics, text, and data analysis. They can allow you to take some pretty heavy data, and funnel it into a simple and eye-catching format. You can put a lot of information into a single infographic, and make it easy for people to reference.

People Love Them

While the reasons are still debatable, it is certain that infographics are very likely to be viewed, shared, and saved by users. Statistics often speak more loudly than opinions and images, so people tend to trust them. Combine this with colorful graphics and smart subtitles — and you have a winning combination.

Create Your Own Infographics

Unlike some other types of images, infographics are mostly just data and icons. You can get away with using stock icons, or just make simple ones yourself. Take a look at some popular infographics that you come across, and get some inspiration for making your own. Be sure to place you blog's name and link somewhere on your infographics.

Section IV – Monetization – The reason you probably came

Building a list still reigns supreme

List building has been around for longer than the Internet, and longer than computers, and, well … a very long time. While you might know all about them, people have probably told you that list building is dead.

Why would people say this? Email is relatively ancient, compared to many of the ways that people interact in the digital world — but it's just as popular as ever, and probably even more so today. If you want to create a basis of followers, you need to add to your list.

Lists Give Mobility

Even if you decide to take down your blog one day, and start something new, your list will ensure that you can contact all of your fans and tell them. No matter what platform you decide to use, your list will be easy to access.

If you want to advertise a product that have started to sell, which relates to your blog, your list is also highly valuable.

How to Make Your List

You should start by collecting the emails and names of people who contact your, and members of your blog. Be careful not to send spam to people though. It is also a good idea to make sure that people actually want to be on your list, so make it easy for them to be removed, should they wish to do so.

Affiliate marketing is a great way to earn

Are you making money by using affiliate marketing on your blog? If not, you might be missing out on a whole lot of income. There are countless bloggers out there who are wildly popular, but still make zero-to-little money from their efforts. If other people are earning with their blogs, why shouldn't you start to do so too?

What is Affiliate Marketing?

Basically, affiliate programs reward people for increasing sales for companies. Have you ever read a review about a new pair of headphones you've been thinking of buying? Chances are that there was at least one link to a place, like Amazon, where you could go to purchase that product. In addition, it's likely that the reviewer would receive a percentage of money, if you did follow that link and buy those headphones. That is affiliate marketing.

It Helps Your Viewers

You don't need to try and sell things that nobody wants, or become an unpopular spammer. If you are already recommending products and services to people, you should take advantage of any affiliate programs that those companies might offer. Not only does it put money in your pocket, but it makes it easier for people to get their hands on the products that you post about. It really is a win-win situation.

It is Seamless

Unlike banner advertisements and popups, affiliate links can be integrated with your content. You're probably placing links to products anyway, so why not use affiliate links that can earn you some money? Most people will not know, or care, that you are advertising, because they actually want what is being sold.

Have you thought about selling your own product?

You might be selling products made by other people, or advertising them for a profit — but have you given any thought to creating your own product to sell through your blog?

What Can You Sell?

Creating your own product might seem like an impossible task, and you might never have given it a thought. Consider this: you have already created a blog, or you are in the process of doing so (even by reading this information, you have set the wheels in motion). Your blog is like a digital product that you need to create yourself, so you are capable of making one.

Create Your Own Ebook

You don't need to invent the next popular gadget. You might choose to create your own ebook, full of the useful information and opinions that you share on your blog. People might be willing to pay money for an easy-to-access version of your content.

Selling Software

Digital products are often the easiest to work with for bloggers, because they already live in a digital world (perhaps for more hours a day than they'd care to admit). Software, such as apps, is another popular type of product that you can sell. If you're useless at programming, it might be a good idea to hire someone to create your software for you.

People Trust You

If you have a blog that is at least slightly popular, there are probably people who trust what you have to say. Within your niche, some people might even view you as an authority. Does that mean that they are more likely to buy a product that you've created, instead of something a total stranger is selling? You can bet it does!

Advertisement space

If your blog generates a lot of hits each day, there are probably companies out there who would like to buy advertisement space from you.

How to Find Buyers

The most basic way to sell advertising space on your blog is to find buyers. This can be as simple as using your blog to tell people that you are willing to sell your space. Make this seem official and organized; don't just write that you're thinking about letting people advertise on your blog. Instead, create your own advertisement, with the details. It might be a good idea to list the prices and types of advertisements on offer. This will encourage people to choose you, and it will show them that you are professional.

Promotional Kits

Another way to find advertisement buyers is to send out promo kits, also known as media kits. These are just documents that tell people about what you're offering, why they should choose your blog for their ads, and perhaps give some testimonials from people who have found your service to be of use.

Take some times to make your promo kit look good, and making it a PDF file is a good idea. Include your blog's name and logo, images, and examples of the advertisements that you can create.

Adding a membership site

One of the hardest parts about running a blog is knowing when you need to take things to the next level. It might seem like a great idea to add memberships to your blog, but doing so too soon might alienate your followers. Often, people consider the act of asking for money to be a greedy, as though you should just work for free, and be glad to do so.

Standing at the Crossroad

If you're thinking about creating paid content, you really are at a crossroad in your blogging journey. Down one path, there is what you are already doing: keeping your blog going, and maintaining the popularity that you already have. Down the other path is something new, and possibly risky: moving into the realm of professional blogging. To operate a membership-only site, your content had better be good, and you need to put in plenty of time and effort. If members feel that they are not getting enough value to justify your fees — they might stop trusting you.

Testing the Waters

Before you dive in and add a membership site to your blog, take a look at your statistics. If people are subscribing, there's a good chance they would be willing to pay a reasonable fee for membership. What about your unsubscribe rates? If people are choosing to stop receiving your content, they most likely weren't getting what they wanted from your blog. That's a good sign that you are not ready to create paid memberships yet.

Take a look at more than just your daily hits. If you are getting plenty of traffic, it could just mean that your SEO tactics are working well, or you might even be getting lucky. It's vital that you can confirm, with real data, that your membership plan is going to be viable to users.

Offer consulting if it suits you

If people are starting to truly value your opinions, and you find yourself regularly giving advice — maybe it's time that you started to offer consultations.

What is Consulting?

Having a successful blog means that you must know a lot about your niche. Some people might like to know just how you made your blog so popular. They might also like some help within that niche.

Suppose that you produce delightful figurines, and you have a blog that tells people how to make them, and contains images of your creations. Do you think that other sellers of figurines might be willing to pay for some advice about their own products? That would be consulting, and it can earn you a lot of money.

Does it Suit You?

Do you love to work with other people? Is helping others something that you're willing to do? Can you articulate your thoughts and opinions well (if you're a blogger, you probably do)? If you've answered yes to these questions, offering your services as a consultant probably suits you. Otherwise, it could be an area to avoid, or you might damage your reputation.

How Much Should You Charge?

This is really your decision, but you can only charge as much as people are willing to pay. When you're just starting out, it is best to keep your fees low, in case you realize that consulting isn't your thing. Once you establish yourself, however, you can really charge as much as people think is fair.

Section IV – Bonus Section

Networking with other bloggers

Networking on the Internet is a lot different than doing it in person. While you are basically doing similar things, the methods that you use, and the way that you carry yourself, are extremely different.

It's Not Faking

To become successful at networking, you are going to need to become a particular type of person, at least when you are networking. Some people think of this as being a fraud, but you are just trying to expose the best aspects of yourself. Creating a positive image is the best way to increase the chance that other bloggers will want to add you to their own networks.

Use the Right Mind-set

To network with other bloggers, you need to form the right sort of mentality. Here are some great tips on how you can do so:

1). **Respect other bloggers.** You should never assume that people are stupid, or that their time isn't as valuable as your own. If you treat people poorly, why should they want to stay in contact with you?
2). **Create win-win interactions.** Even if you are great at pretending, people are probably going to learn what you really want from them. When you contact someone with a request, make it worthwhile for them. It's okay if they know that you want something, as long as you are willing to give something in return.
3). **Be honest.** If you want something, don't be afraid to ask for it right away. If you have a proposition that's valuable to everyone involved, people shouldn't mind your honesty. Never attempt to manipulate people; it's unethical, and nobody wants to work with a liar.

How to Build Your Network

Now that you know how to properly conduct yourself in the world of bloggers, it's time to make a network of your own. Begin by commenting on people's blogs, and starting a conversation. Creating friends is an ideal way to build your network.

If you are going to cold-contact people who you don't know, be polite and to-the-point. This is going to be the first contact that you have with them, so try to make a good impression.

Attending blogging events is a great way to get out there and mingle with other people in your market. Remember to keep a good mind-set, and try to be at least a little charismatic.

Additional Traffic Sources

Traffic is like the lifeblood of your blog; without it, you might as well be throwing your content into the trash, because either way — no one is going to see it. You should also build multiple ways to get traffic, so that you're not spreading yourself too thin. How can you learn how to create additional sources of traffic, and maximize the number of hits that your blog gets?

Know Your Traffic Statistics

Before you can really build up your traffic, you should know how many visits you're already receiving. Your blogging platform, whatever it is, probably has a built-in tool that will tell you what you need to know. Become familiar with your traffic trends, and check them daily.

Organic Visits

You might have heard about "organic" traffic, but what exactly it it? When someone uses a search engine, and the results lead them to your blog — that is organic traffic. It is especially valuable, but

pretty hard to get (unless you are using great SEO). While search engines are important, you shouldn't rely on them alone.

Pay for Advertising

This is a great way to go, provided that you have a big enough budget. There are loads of different sites that let people buy advertising space, so choose the ones that you think will bring you the most valuable visitors.

Email Marketing

If you have been creating your own list, it should be easy to use email to bring more people to your blog. Make sure that you link to yourself, and format your emails so they look professional. There are services that make sending out bulk emails simple, and they can actually give you statistics about how well your campaigns are working.

Social Media Marketing

This is probably an obvious one, but that doesn't make it any less important. You can use your social media accounts to direct attention to your blog. Instead of just spamming links, however, you should give people a taste of what your blog is all about — and leave them wanting more.

Conclusion

I would like to thank you for taking the journey through this book with me. I spent countless hours trying to show you exactly what recipe worked for me, because I want you to be prosperous.

The time has come where I cut you loose and you take this thing to the next level. The key is in your hand, all you have to do is unlock your full potential and consequently a passive revenue stream will be unlocked as well.

I wish you the best of luck and I hope to see you on the web soon!